Holding on and looking

out

**A collection of new poems
to be read in bed and shared aloud
by**

David C Johnson

First published 2010 by Paralalia
1, Elgin Park,
Bristol
BS6 6RU
UK

ISBN 978-0-9548117-6-1

The right of David C Johnson to be identified as
author of this work has been asserted in
accordance with section 77 of the Copyright,
Designs and Patents Act 1988

A CIP copy of this book is available from the
British Library

Cover front illustration from an etching
© David C Johnson
Cover back photograph by Crysse Morrison
Designed by Paralalia

Printed by Short Run Press Exeter

Dedication

This book is for my wife, Alex, who supports me always, and those many friends who have encouraged me.

Contents

Ear Trumpets

Close by the Arnolfini
Stands Pero's Bridge,
Which spans the water.
It has two grey wing-like things,
Its counterweights.
Some think that they are horns,
Like the devil's horns
Or horns of some fantastic beast.
But when I see them,
I think of ear-trumpets
Placed there for Pero,
The slave who first set foot in England
Two hundred years and more ago.
So that now his soul can listen
To the sounds of the docks today.

The sirens wailing on Saturday nights
Rushing to rescue the flailing
Drunk, who has tumbled in the water;
The uninvited samba band
In frothy pink with whistles shrieking;
Loudspeakers blaring from the ferries,
Whose Captains tell of Bristol's history;
The giggling girls in hip high skirts
That do no more than fringe their thongs;
The sniggering boy-o's, who try their luck
With all the charm of Michael Winner;
The black-clad bouncers blocking doors
To bars and clubs and gambling dens.
"You can't come in - **you** are barred.
I told you before, you're barred.
Not you darling or you

You can come in anytime.
But **you** are barred. Yes you!"
The buskers, hustlers, market traders;
The Acrobats in skimpy panties
With saucy chat and sparklers sparkling
From their back-sides as they pose;
The clubbers leaving "happy hours"
Louder but more prone to spark;
The gutters chuckling with their urine
Too pissed to wait for somewhere dark;

The grey-haired cyclist in her lycra
Approaching tourists sotto voce,
Proffering her vegan flapjacks;
The Big Issue seller's needy pleading;
The squealing friends, who coincide
Minutes since they last collided;
Diving sea-gulls screaming hunger,
As they squabble over junk food
Jettisoned by passing hulks;
The bump and grind of skateboard tricksters
Going for that extra "air";
The steam train wheezing on the dock-side,
On a track that leads nowhere.

How different from those earlier sounds
That Pero must have heard,
When he first stepped on Bristol soil,
Servant slave of Mr. Pinney.
Then sweaty dockers teemed the wharves
Unloading cane and best Virginia.
The pubs were filled with scurvy sea-dogs
Telling tales of death and mermaids.
Whilst merchants counted up their guineas,

A jingling wealth so cruelly won
From the devil's trade triangle.
Then the ships were moored alongside
Far into the city centre.
Now all paved and covered over
With decking and trite water-features.
Then the breezes strummed the rigging
And played a one note melody.
Now there's shushing and a-gushing
Of cafés, frothing up their coffees
And in the air the constant rumble
Of traffic noise, today's backbeat.

But sometimes, if you listen hard,
The sounds of Africa float by,
When a white-robed, black musician
Sits and plucks his trusty kora,
Cascading notes from Old Benin,
Melodies from Mauritania,
Memories for Pero's soul.

Bristol 2009

I have lived in Bristol for twenty-five years
And each day that I'm here, I learn something
more,
Discover new places and meet new people.
We live in our little corners,
Never venturing too far.
Sometimes we're surprised by a building or tree
That we notice for the first time,
 A few streets from home.

There are parts of Bristol
That we **know** are unsafe,
Dangerous, much too scary to visit.
And how do we know this,
When we're mostly at home?
We have read it in the Evening Post.
We've heard it on the news.
We've spoken to a friend
And he has been told for certain - fact !
That you shouldn't go there,
Wherever "there" is.

South across the river
To the Hartcliffe "badlands".
East to the no-man's-land
In Lockleaze or Greenbank.
West to Lawrence Weston,
Where walking in the parks
Makes you feel nervous of
Young lads on the swings,
Because you can't help thinking
That they might swing at you

North West to the "nice" parts,
Stoke Bishop and Sneyd Park.
Where they worry about St.John,
Whose birthday was last Friday.
He's four and cannot read a word.
They anguish over Kate
In case, she's "in the club"
And fails her A-levels.
How will they face their neighbours?
They "stress" about their pension pot.
Will it melt away like snow?

Since I came to Bristol all those years ago,
New peoples have come, communities have grown.
Diasporas daring to be seen and heard.
Looked down on by everyone,
A hierarchy of disdain,
But gradually making their mark on the town.
Some have come for ever and some for respite.
New Poles don't go to the Old Poles' Polish club.
They're saving to buy their own house in Krakow.
Other incomers are sucked into squalor,
Living their lives on the boundaries of crime,
Left at the back in a classroom daze,
Too big too admit that they haven't a clue.
And in the City Centre, studio-apartments
Ring the dock-side with en-suite showers.
But there's not much for low rent,
Not much for the poor,
For that you go to Southmead, Easton, St.Paul's.

By the Dockside rises
A glass and metal box.
The new Museum of Bristol
To be filled with things that were,
When Bristol was a city
That made buses, cranes and planes;
Whole planes and not just wings;
Motorbikes that raced on the Isle of Man;
Buses, Bristol buses for Bristol Transport Co.;
Shoes for the workers that laboured in the
factories;
Reinforced corsets for their girlfriends and wives;
Helicopters, ships, motorcars and steam-trains.
All were once made in this city of ours:
Ropes and cables;
Leather tanned for handbags;
Leather tanned for shoes;
Cigarettes and packaging,
Billions every year;
And paper bags for sweetmeats,
Fry's and Famous Names.

The Museum of Bristol will reach out to children,
Telling in wonder these tales of the past.
And the knowledge imparters will have read up the
notes,
Written by someone for whom it is a job.
But who next week will turn out a history of
Melbourne,
Norwich, Swindon or even Beijing.
Bristol is a metaphor.

A city that once made things,
Producing less and less.
While the buildings grow for offices
Cafés, bars and shops.

A place where we know that we must do
something,
But cannot agree what that something should be.

Why Bristol is best
(Written at request of BBC Radio Bristol for National poetry Day 2009 to show why Bristol is better than Bath.)

At first I thought to earn your applause,
With a poem done like the football scores.
You know.
Bristol City has Cycleway to Pill- Bath nil.
Bristol City has Cary Grant, Hollywood hero –
Bath zero.
Suspension Bridge over a gorge Bristol has one –
Bath none.
But then I thought no that's petty point scoring,
Just tell them all what makes Bristol not boring.
Like the Docks and the ferries that sail end to end;
Like the fact that you'll always bump into a friend,
When walking the length of Gloucester Road's shops
Or waiting for ages at First Bus's bus-stops;
Like the art on the streets thanks to Ghostboy and Banksy;
The art trails that flourish all over the city;
Live music that's played both classic and gritty;
Festivals of kites, balloons and the sea
Of drama and music and great poetry.
Cathedrals, we've two, which isn't so shabby,
Compared to a single Bath-stone abbey.
Plus we've the fairest church in the land.
But most of all it's the people that's grand.
Such a rich mixture that's so hard to beat,
Often the friendliest you'll ever meet.

Bristolians come from all over the Earth
And it's people who make up our city's true worth.
Bristol is best. No contest!

Elgin Fox

I remember the first time that I saw a fox,
In the middle of Redland Bristol
Late at night.
Its eyes bright beads of night-time bijouterie
Flashing in the sodium glare.
I remember the first time that I saw fox prints
Etched in the lawn's smooth, pre-dawn snow
And the millisecond splash
Of russet brush winking in and out of our privet.
I reported these sightings in full to my loved ones,
Eager to share my Attenborough moments.
In recent years these visits have increased.
Daylight forays along streets and in gardens.
Sniffing the bins at the local "cop-shop".
Looking to dine on criminal waste.
The fox's beauty still captures my eye,
But its manner is now almost brazen.
A visiting friend delights in the sight
And we delight in revealing our Reynard,
Crossing the grass and leaping up onto
Our hand-crafted, English Oak table.
"Aaah, how sweet - How cute,
How lovely - You brute!"
That's disgusting. Revolting. It's pissing
All over the fine-grained surface of our oak table.
He's marking his claim to the territory.
My territory! Our territory! Not his!
"Piss off! Get lost!
Go on, shove off!"

He leaps to the ground and runs to the shed,
Where later I tread in his droppings.
Nature is wondrous. Nature is shit.
Later that week in the twilight gloom,
I opened the back-gates onto the road,
To be met by the stare of the fox
Who was standing in safety,
In our neighbour's front yard.
I knew in an instant what he was thinking.
 "Cheers mate.
Thanks for unlocking the door to my dunny."

From rarity to lavatory. From wonder to disgust.
How fickle are my feelings.
I love:
Nature on the telly; nature in the press;
Nature captured vividly by digital eyes.
But don't let it bite me, sting me or fight me.
Don't let it crap, where I might be eating.
Leave it in the pages of National Geographic.
Send Paris Hilton to wrestle with the crocs.
But keep me at a distance
From that peeing urban fox.

The Severn Beach Line

How hard its band of fans have fought,
To keep the line to Severn Beach
That runs from Bristol Temple Meads.
How doggedly did they beseech
The councillors and fat controllers,
The bureaucrats and city rollers

That trains should never cease to serve
The stations on this unique line.
That runs through cuttings deep and long,
Past houses mean and mansions fine.
That soars on arches over town
And plunges dark 'neath Clifton Down.

That carries hundreds ev'ry day
To work, to school, to see the sights.
Young mothers with their shopping bags,
Who trail their kids like satellites.
Publishers and old professors,
Filing clerks and men's hairdressers,

Commuters on the way to Bath,
Cyclists starting their day's outing,
Texting girls and blazered pupils,
Tilers with a tub of grouting,
All use this rattling diesel train
That shuttles up and down again.

Through Lawrence Hill on busy lines,
Then branching off on single track,
Past builders' yards and junior schools,
Allotments green and terrace backs,
Stapleton Road, Montpelier,
Redland and its station atelier.

Where craftsmen work with cloth and wood,
Restoring chesterfields and chairs,
In the waiting room and office,
Where once the porter had his lair.
All station buildings have been changed.
Their purposes quite rearranged.

On to Clifton and the tunnel,
One mile through Bristol's rock and clay.
Emerging blinking by the Avon
This route now travelled ev'ryday.
Close by Sea Mills, it spans the stream,
Once port for a Roman quinquereme.

Next stop is Shire' , then Avonmouth.
A faded, sometimes lonely place,
Where the yellow smoke from smelters
No longer leaves its grimy trace.
Where turbines turn slow in the breeze
And the cars unshipped are Japanese.

St. Andrews Road is optional,
O'er-topped by crumbling gaunt decay.
Who would ask the train to stop here,
Amongst this dank, concrete array?
Let's hurry to the end of the line
And the terminus, which once stood fine.

Severn Beach, Bristol's own Blackpool,
That's what they said in days gone by.
When the trippers came from Birmingham
To the Blue Lagoon 'neath open sky.
Where bathing beauties smiled and twirled,
In a golden age and a different world.

The Lighthouse

The old lighthouse that once faced Appledore
Was demolished some fifty years ago.
Replaced by a light on the Crow Point shore
That stands unmanned next estuary flow.
One steel-framed beacon alone, when before
Light-keepers in teams kept the lamps aglow.
A few weathered bricks are all that remain.
Reminders of summers I won't see again.

Sailing from Instow on just the right tide,
To land on the foreshore 'neath the old light.
Unloading the kit and all the supplies.
Trudging the beach to find the best site.
Impatient to climb the dunes for a slide,
On printed tin trays that went fast as flight.
When the estuary ebb unveiled the rocks,
We'd pull on our plimsolls, jettison socks.

The pools, their prawns and other attractions
Called to us, "grab up your catch bag and net".
This was the highlight of our day's actions.
The fam'ly prawning, a fisher's quartet.
That first dip and scoop, those first extractions,
The inquiring shouts of:" what did you get?"
Answered by: "Prawns! Thousands!" "I've caught
an eel!"
Ingredients of the forthcoming meal.

The slap of the cloth bag tied round my waist.
The faint stab of whiskers pricking my thigh.
Indignant green fish escaping in haste,
From the scrape of my net, as it trawled by.
Then tiring at last my steps were retraced,
Back to the picnic and bacon-egg pie.
The laying of driftwood for the camp-fire.
The playing with matches, my heart's desire!

A battered old saucepan filled to the brim.
Its tidal-race waters brought to the boil.
Our catch bags emptied and the prawns tipped in,
Jade green to pink, as they slipped their coil.
Though years may vanish and memories dim,
I'll never forget those feasts so royal,
Washed down with squash and seasoned with
sand.
What need of spices from Samarkand?

Picnic consumed and the tide now turning,
We'd re-board the skiff and ready its sails.
Summer over and rekindled yearning,
To come back next year whatever prevails.
Lighthouse adventures already burning
Their images into my little grey cells.
Ten summers, long ago, spanned that golden age.
Yet often they grace my mind centre stage.

On Baggy Point

The smell of the gorse,
The wheel of the hawk,
Tawny brown 'gainst lichened cliff.
Fulmars nesting in their rock slums.
And I am shinning the look-out post.
Holding on and looking-out.
Vertigo cliff edge,
Crumble of earth rocks,
Surfers paddling towards the horizon.
The sea is a millpond bereft of rollers.
Lundy is sinking before my eyes,
Swallowed by mist and imagination.

In a Swanage Tea-shop

Lunchtime and two shrunken friends,
Shoulders drooped to table level,
Tuck into veg and gravy.
Two hats oscillating,
In time with their masticating.
One is red in tight-knit wool,
Worn like a dollop of "raspberry sauce"
On a swirl of Softee ice-cream.
The other a jaunty green, peaked cap,
As favoured by Princess Anne,
In nineteen seventy-three.
Sporadic chat of this and that.
Inquiries of the waitress
About the Apple Cake.
"It's tasty, light, and cinnamony,"
She assures them both.

What were you two up to,
When your locks were blonde
And Princess Anne was a Page One
Fashion icon?

Meadowsweet

She was Meadowsweet,
Spread amongst the Lady's Bedstraw.
Sacred to the ancient Druids,
Tasting like a summer honey,
With a smell
That makes hearts merry.
Come to me my Meadowsweet.
Slip your Lady's Smock.
Lay amongst the Thyme with me,
Your lovesome Ragged Robin.

How to communicate with a worm

No matter how much I tell them not to,
They still do it.
Each evening, as the sun sets and the dew falls,
They creep inside,
Under the front door, over the welcome mat,
With its smiling porcupine motif,
Tiny wire-thin red worms from the compost bin.
Why do they ignore me?
It isn't as if I don't feed them.
I do. Strips of apple peel,
Long enough to spell my name; carrot tops;
Printed paper cartons; a feast
For any self-respecting worm.
Each evening I gather them up,
In the palm of my hand and return them
To their home.
I am not sure that I will ever discover
How to communicate with a worm.

Jungle Night

I have walked in the jungle at night,
As darkness fell like a black-out curtain.
I have slept in the jungle at night,
Listening to the slithering of what, I was not
certain.
I've had leeches suck me in the jungle at night
And felt the squelching of my blood in my boot.
I've had cockroaches visit in the jungle at night,
Entering the pockets of my smart safari suit.
I have woken in the jungle at night,
The cries of large beasts all too close to where I lay.
I have risen at the dawn of jungle night,
As the whoops of troops of gibbons welcomed in
the day.

In general, that is why I prefer to wake up
In my Victorian semi in Redland.

All I want is less

All I want is less -
Less inches round my waist
Less junk in ev'ry room
Less doing things in haste
Less bust that follows boom
Less weekly household bills
Less tension in the land
Less anger over-spills
Less laughter that is canned
Less green-fly on my beans
Less I don't understand
Less disenchanted teens
Less dog dirt in the sand
Less aches ev'ry morning
Less reality TV
Less wrinkles when yawning
Less disrespect for trees-
All I want is less.
I can't ask for anything more.

Speaking

Don't judge me by the way that I speak.
Don't rule me out because I sound sleek,
Like a Tory MP or a Dimbleby
Or low-grade aristocracy.
To you I may seem la-di-da,
Like a toff who loves the opera,
But I'm not! I love Dolly and Johnny
And Willie. I love Country
& Western and I love Hill-billy.

My voice is a cover that hides a book,
Which underneath is not how it looks.
My mind is ineffectual,
No perpetual intellectual.
Philosophy is not for me.
I prefer a mystery,
By Christie, Doyle not Wittengenstein.
I don't read Proust, that's not my line,
For me a thriller will do just fine,

Years ago they used to mimic me,
When I was a teacher in Oswestry.
They modified their border tones,
That Karen Thomas and Nerys Jones.
"Good morning Sir", "How are we today?"
Then they would wait to see what I'd say:
A tilt of head and a smirk on their lips,
As pleased as punch with these witty quips.
Whilst I glared at them, hands on my hips.

Sometimes I feel that the way that I talk,
Has hindered me, because people baulk
At the thought of my standing in front of a crowd,
In Easton or Hartcliffe and talking out loud,
In a way that will not patronize.
Because like it or not, we do stigmatize,
Through accents, looks, a limp hand-shake,
Eye contact missing, some social mistake.
An unfortunate twitch, that's all it need take.

I know that I'm at a disadvantage,
As a poet standing up on the stage.
When the person before has an Irish Brogue,
So light and bewitching, a leprechaun rogue,
Who makes merest doggerel sound like Yeats,
Who can sweep you up and open the gates
To a kingdom of verses that maybe balls.
Yet you're a prisoner in the marble halls
Of his accent and voice, as it floats and falls.

And the same goes for that Highland lilt
Or the Summerset burr of Acker Bilk.
And as for the patois from Kingston Jamaica,
What chance me got when he choose to take a
Verse about Reggae or Yardies or ackee.
Do you see what I mean? My voice is lacking
That sunny charm or emerald fancy.
I'd have to rely on necromancy
To win first prize against them, you see.

There is just one consolation for me,
I could read the news on the BBC.

Mature Love

It seems to me that the young of today
Are inured in everyway,
To images of spilling guts
And deaths by a thousand cuts.
They lap it up in X-box games
That feature violence that maims.
They drink it in from plasma screens,
Those close-up clips of torture scenes.
And when exposed to hard-core porn,
They flip channels and simply yawn.
They find it hard to be impressed,
By sweaty heaving naked chests.

But tell them that their Mum and Dad,
Frequently have sex unclad.
These little darlings blanch and wail
That this has gone beyond the pale.
Describe how Mum loves Dad to mount her,
On the marbled kitchen counter,
Writhing in the breakfast debris,
Shrieking out in ecstasy.
Those apathetic, hard-nosed offspring
Show outrage at such rogering.

Now I admit that when you're young,
The thought of doing it for fun,
Much past the age of forty-one,
Does require imagination.
The idea of copulation

Between the aged of our nation,
And more than that, between ones folks!
That's sick fantasy beyond a joke.

Yet it does happen frequently,
Tenderly, energetically:
Despite those extra waistline inches;
Despite needing bathroom winches;
Despite those drooping bits and boobs;
The furring up of ventricle tubes;
The unnerving shortness of breath;
The fear of post-coital death.
Yes, despite all this, it is does go on,
Way past the age of forty-one!

Of Dyson men

"If you want more sex, do the dishes .....
women find men more attractive, if they pick up a
duster, say researchers from the University of
California".
The Times March 8, 2008

The time is right to talk of Dyson-men,
Upright, bag-free, cyclone-driven males,
Gatherers of fluff and clippings of nails.
They have heard it on the News at Ten
That helping with the housework gets you laid.
Researchers from the USA have made
A claim that women respond better, when

Men take up their share of household tasks.
It seems that women are keener to lust,
After partners who are willing to dust,
Before removing their G-strings and basques.
They like a man with impregnated wipes,
Who battles with dirt to earn his stripes,
Before donning his handcuffs and masks.

That sweet aroma of *Pledge* in the air
Will excite her more than Eau de Cologne.
She won't be able to leave him alone.
Yet the dusting man is not without care.
He knows that macho mates may ridicule
Him with comments barbed and beastly cruel,
As they slump on sofas with glassy stare.

Watching the telly, in beer-stained attire,
Amongst a foul nest of discarded snacks,
Fast-food wrappers, remains of six-packs.
Sneering that males with dusters are dire
Specimens lost to the cause of real men,
Who can attract a woman as and when,
Because real men set women afire.

But what those paunchy chauvinists ignore,
Is that whilst they brag of the sex they once had
And how in the past they drove women mad,
Dyson-men do it now, down on the floor,
In every room, satisfaction guaranteed.
No more humiliating need to plead.
When they finish the chores they know they'll
score.

So remember, you men, who won't lift a finger,
It's unlikely that women will want to linger
With you and your slovenly, slothful charms.
They'll prefer the warmth of Dyson-man's arms.

*As someone who does the housework, the only
trouble is that I am often too tired to respond to
my wife's demands*

The Credit Cruncher

In Gloucester Road, the Pound Shop's
Become the Credit Cruncher.
Another sign that none will stop
This economic puncture.
The fizz is going flat.
The lights are going out.
Woolworth's now a blackened tooth
In the High Street's down-turned pout.

And "WasNow" is the chorus,
Repeated in each window.
Heartfelt offers that implore us
Buy! Now prices are so low.
Was one hundred twenty.
Now reduced to sixty.
One by one the boards go up:
"To let" - call Neil or Christie.

But who will lease these spaces,
These bleak and echoing voids?
Which brave souls will take the places
Of businesses foreclosed by Lloyds
And other banks as bad?
Is a banker's conscience rent,
As he seeks to repossess
The cash he freely lent?

Encouraged in the good times
To borrow to the hilt,
Businesses go belly up.
Do bankers feel the guilt?

The sheep that safely grazed

They are knocking down the factories, one by one,
To construct new apartments for everyone.
When all the plants are flattened?
When every line is stilled?
Who will make the bricks,
That the builders need to build?

They are grubbing up the green belt, field by field,
For new towns and shopping malls,
Mammon unconcealed.
When all the trees are bulldozed?
When every hedge is razed?
Which shopper will remember,
The sheep that safely grazed?

Edith Piaf sang of no regrets

Edith Piaf sang of no regrets.
The Marlboro Man died from cigarettes.
And I, I mean me,
I wanted to be a protester up a threatened tree.
To be chained to Greenham's fence in nineteen
eighty-three.
Regrets? Yes, I've a few,
When I think of all the things that I didn't do.
But when I write down in a list
Of all those things that I missed
And compare that to the list of things I've done.
The latter list is longer
And the latter was more fun.
Looking back and regretting
Is no better than blood-letting,
As a cure for Yellow fever
Or a toothache reliever.
So when you're tempted to protest
That your choices weren't the best.
Don't!
But do -
Put your hand to the plough.
Use your energies now,
For today and tomorrow,
Not yesterday's sorrow.
Don't let the day get older.
Lift that weight from your shoulder.
The future is what matters.
The past is disappearing

And it's no use steering,
Whilst continually peering
In your rear-view mirror.

Rubbish haiku

Kamikatsu is a village that wants to be the first zero-waste community in Japan.

In Kamikatsu,
They've no time for renga or haiku.
Their lives are devoted to rubbish recycu.

In this Japanese village, every item they chuck,
Is washed and graded and not treated like muck.
How different from China, where they don't give a
Quarter as much time to solving the problem of
waste.

The Limeriku
There was an old lady from Kamikatsu
Who lived up to her elbows in clammy rats' poo,
As she sorted her waste into thirty four streams
And mused "it's funny: how life seldom mirrors
ones dreams."

Three cheap mousses
A true incident on the streets of Bristol

This crazy-looking man comes up to me and asks:
"Do you want to help?"

"I want to lock up my bike." I reply.

"Do you want to help me?" he persists.

I finish locking up my bike and say;
"What kind of help do you need?"

He looks me earnestly in the eye and says:
"You know that Sainsbury shop, just down the
road?"
He points vaguely behind him.

"Yes, I know it." I respond and nod my head for
emphasis.

"Well the thing is. The thing is, they've got a
special offer at the moment. Its three mousses for
99p. The thing is. The thing is, I'm skint. Could
you spare me a pound? I'm really starving."

How could I refuse? Living on the streets, begging
for a living, likely to starve, if he didn't get those
three mousses."

"Here you are mate."
"Cheers."

Button slogans for poetry buffs

Slam Punk

I'm a poet: be my friend

Bard arse

Poets against

Is it all a bad dream?

Pre-published poet

I like it doggerel fashion

Help me: I'm a poet

I've gone metric

Woke up this morning. Damn!

Take a hike you!

I'm the poet Laurie ate

Rhyming? Don't see the pint

Sonnet Boom!

Let me read your metre

Have I got clerihews for you!

Anyone for Tennyson?

Poetry saved my life

Dylan Thomas was Welsh

I can do it for three minutes

Dave Shocks

It was a sharp and acrid smell
That warned them, all was not so well.
And when they peered around his door,
To where they'd seen him hours before,
All that remained of Dave was socks.
He'd been vaporised by voltage shocks,
Caused by his innate desire
To fiddle with electric wire.
"We told him he would end up dead",
Was what his mum and dad had said,
When questioned by the local priest.
"He was a most ungrateful beast.
Would he listen? Not in the least.
It quite puts you off this child-rearing
To find they can be so un-fearing
Of everything you've warned about.
It makes us want to stamp and shout.
When we think of all the money spent.
How he would nag, so we'd relent
And buy him things he didn't need.
And then ignore us when we'd plead:
Not to poke things in the sockets,
Because he'd get a nasty shock. It's
Disappointing. It really is.
It's got us both in quite a tizz
That Dave could leave us quite like this.
So parents who have kids like Dave,
Try not to let them misbehave.
It's made us both feel very stressed
To know that though we tried our best,
There's nothing left to lay to rest
Of Dave, the irritating pest."

Don't be so silly David

I do not recall much washing at school.
A weekly splash, in the bathroom upstairs,
Overseen by matron, in her starched, cool
Linen apron. Four cast-iron tubs in pairs

Occupied by pre-pubescent confreres.
Not one pubic hair to crown our jewels.
Our grubby towels draped on backs of chairs.
I do not recall much washing at school.

'Though there was no line 'round the bath, the rule
Was five inches deep. Any more earned glares
From matron enthroned on her cork-lined stool.
A weekly splash, in the bathroom upstairs

Was sometimes a moment for silent prayers
That my flaccid penis would not unspool.
For bath-night was no time to attract stares.
Overseen by matron, in her starched, cool

Apron, who'd bark out, "stop playing the fool"
"Don't be so silly", as one's stiffness flared.
How I did rue my recalcitrant tool.
Linen apron, four cast-iron tubs in pairs

Small details from a time of few cares,
Before the Jacuzzi and spa-whirlpool.
Nice boys protected from worldly affairs.
Was it really so, were we spared the cruel?
I do not recall.

The Reverend Bromwich

The Reverend Bromwich is now long dead,
Nash Metropolitan owner-driver.
Unorthodox wheels, when all's said and done,
For an Anglican priest in 'sixty-one.
Favoured boys were invited to tread
Up the stairs to his room on the second floor,
At Winchester Lodge Preparatory School.
There he'd converse with them, as a rule,
Give them a sweet and a stroke on the leg,
Bare skin below the hem of their shorts.
Reports in the dorm would later reveal,
How high his hand had ventured to steal.
Discreetly dismissed, tossed out with the dregs,
His reign of candy and timid caresses
Was brief,   .
One term,
Before he was hist'ry,
Like the subject he taught us so dismally.
Today I recall him so much better,
Than facts about the Treaty of Breda,
Which long since have faded away.

Entering the Turkish Baths

The Turkish Baths in Istanbul
Are three centuries old.
And I, at three score years,
Am entering them for the first time.
Shyly I strip to my fundamentals,
A thin cloth to wind around my waist.
My spectacles steam,
As I lie on the marble
And anxiously sweat,
Whilst my bath-house attendant awaits.
He is four square,
Built like the ramparts of Constantinople.
His bare chest a thick mat
Of darkest sprung curls.
His moustaches luxuriant as Saddam Hussein's.
I limply submit to the massage and rub,
And muse that this is where it all started
To go wrong for Rock Hudson.

Henry the Eighth and his many wives

Henry the Eighth and his many wives,
All had a liking for thin-diced chives.
In addition, he thought it silly
To eat cooked food that had no chili.
He often declared a menu weak,
If it did not mention fenugreek.

Kate Aragon was no paragon,
When it came to wanting tarragon.
And as for her desire for cumin,
King Hal would often find her fumin'
That her meals lacked bite and savour.
So soon fell she from Henry's favour.

Queen Anne Boleyn, Henry's second fling,
Spent much of her time in dallying.
A courtier heard her murmur, "Nick,
Sprinkle my oysters with turmeric"
They say she whispered, "try harder Tom
I must have plenty of cardamom"

Whilst Ann of Cleeves rubbed fresh bay leaves
Over her face and under her sleeves,
Because she thought that it was unfair
That Henry called her his Flanders mare.
This herby treatment did her no good.
Henry divorced her because he could.

Now Katherine Howard and Katherine Parr
They loved tandoori masala.
But Katy H loved more than spices
And so when left to her devices,
She winked and flirted brazenly.
Then lost her head quite brutally.

Of all his wives, Hal found Jane the tops,
For he loved her way with mutton chops,
On which she crushed fresh coriander.
A taste which made his hands meander
Amongst Miss Seymour's lacy trappings,
A prelude to her full unwrapping.

And so here ends this nonsense rhyme,
About King Henry, herbs and spouses.
I hope you have enjoyed the thyme,
Learning how spiced food arouses.

Cherry Now

It is not a secret.
I am not ashamed.
My age in two weeks can be named.

I will be sixty.
The party invitations are in hand.
The wine is ordered.
The entertainment planned.
And 'til yesterday,
I felt pretty good,
Like any healthy, fifty-nine year old should.
But the nearer the day,
The greater my fears,
The more I regret those three score years.

The free bus pass application is in.
The nice woman in the Office
Used no spin.
She didn't say: "You look too young".
Just "Do you need big print?"
And that stung.
My work pension has started
And that's weird.
Every month a sum appearing
In my bank account,
Without effort.

It ought to be a comfort.
It should put me at my ease.
But more and more I think of
Housman's "Loveliest of Trees"
How "fifty springs *were* little room"
For his Lad of twenty
"To look at things in bloom".

I never used to count my summers.
They came and went without a care.
What was left undone in August,
Could always wait until next year.
Now I am not so sure.
I fret and wonder,
How many summers more
Can I expect,
Before my body is too wrecked
To tackle dreams;
To tick off lists
Of things to do "one day".

One day, that's all it is,
From fifty-nine to sixty
And yet it seems
To draw a line,
To build a wall,
Whence there is no turning back.